MW00422731

Table of Contents

Chapter One

Love Defined

The English language can be somewhat stunted in the sense that we often use one word to describe an action which inherently has a variety of applications. For example, we use the word "love" universally to apply to any object and any level of feeling. We love God, we love our spouse, we love our children, we love pizza, we love football, we love going on vacations, and we love our friends. This broad word usage in the English language can result in a slightly incomplete understanding of certain teachings in the bible because the original languages of Hebrew and Greek invariably will utilize several different words to describe something which in English is covered by only one word. As a first step to understanding what God teaches about love and marriage, we must realize the English translations do not always adequately reflect the unique, varying meanings and intent of the Author when it comes to a word such as "love". For this reason, it is vital to establish firm definitions for the diverse uses of the word "love" which God uses throughout Scripture. As a quick examination of relevant terminology within the parameters of marriage, it will suffice for us to survey five different Greek "love" words and one Hebrew "love" word, because doing so will shed great light on what God intends us to understand about the marriage relationship.

Greek Terms:

1) **Epithumia** – Strong desire; to set the heart on, long for; when practiced wrongly it becomes *to lust or to covet:*

   a. *Therefore God also gave them up to uncleanness, in the lusts [epithumia] of their hearts, to dishonor their bodies among themselves (Romans 1:24)*

2) **Eros** – Romantic love, passionate, sentimental, yearning to unite with and possess the beloved; emotional feeling-based love, it is changeable and cannot last all by itself. Eros is not used in the New Testament but the meaning is expressed in several passages of The Song of Solomon, for example:

a. *May he kiss me with the kisses of his mouth! For your love is better than wine. Your oils have a pleasing fragrance, your name is like purified oil; Therefore the maidens love you. Draw me after you and let us run together! The king has brought me into his chambers... (Song of Solomon 1:2-4)*

3) **Storge** – comfortable, familiar, natural affection, belonging type of love; characterized as familial love – shared by spouses, parents, children and siblings. This form is combined with Phileo (brotherly love) in the following verse:

a. *Let love be without hypocrisy. Abhor what is evil. Cling to what is good. 10 Be kindly affectionate [philostorge]to one another with brotherly love, in honor giving preference to one another; (Romans 12:9,10)*

4) **Phileo** – cherishes and has tender affection but always expects response. A love relationship typified by comradeship, brotherhood, sharing, communication, and friendship.

a. *So when they had eaten breakfast, Jesus said to Simon Peter, "Simon, son of Jonah, do you love [agapao] Me more than these? He said to Him, "Yes, Lord; You know that I love [phileo] You." (John 21:15)*

5) **Agape** – Values, serves, and gives unconditionally; a love of action and of will. Charity. It is the love God manifested for us when He sent His Son to die for us. It is a love concerned with doing what is best for the beloved, regardless of response. Its source is Jesus Christ. It can be fueled by nothing less than the Holy Spirit and cannot be completely understood by the unsaved world.

a. *For God so loved [agapao] the world that He gave His only begotten Son, that whoever believes in Him should not perish but have everlasting life. (John 3:16)*

Hebrew Term:

1) **Ahava** – the Old Testament counterpart to Agape, the Hebrew word Ahava is made up of 3 Hebrew letters, aleph, hey, and vet. From these root letters comes a

root word, hav, which means "to give".
All forms of this word carry the
implication of an act of giving from
within ourselves toward another. It is
the purposeful, servanthood love of the
spirit and the will, unconditionally
committed to seeking what is best for the
beloved at all times, expressed through
spiritual, emotional, and physical
channels:

    a. *You shall not take vengeance, nor
       bear any grudge against the children
       of your people, but you shall love
       (ahava) your neighbor as yourself: I
       am the Lord. (Leviticus 19:18)*
    b. *Since you were precious in My sight,
       You have been honored, And I have
       loved (ahab) you; Therefore I will give
       men for you, And people for your life.
       (Isaiah 43:4)*

The above list of words for love is by no
means exhaustive of every type of love in either
the Greek or Hebrew languages, but contains
the ones most relevant to the subject of
marriage. God has created many specific levels
of love in which all of humanity can engage, but
there is a special, foundational love which must

be practiced within the marriage relationship if it is to be the blessing and gift God meant it to be. Unfortunately, because English is so limited and modern society is so far removed from knowing God and what the Bible teaches, people today simply have no understanding of the subject.

We know our Creator is the Author of order and not confusion, therefore it is imperative to examine which particular original language word is used in marriage-focused Bible passages using the word "love". By looking up the Greek or Hebrew words we can more accurately realize the true intent of any specific verse or command. Ultimately what becomes clear is the primary type of love necessary in marriage is that of "agape" or "ahava" love. All other forms of love in a marital relationship can only thrive when agape love is the foundation. Since God's marriage instructions to the church are found in the New Testament, I will primarily focus on the Greek word "agape" in this book, rather than the Old Testament Hebrew word "ahava".

As we begin to understand more deeply the meaning of agape love we can then realize how and why so many marriages fail today. *My people are destroyed for lack of knowledge. (Hosea*

4:6) How often are marriages destroyed because spouses do not have the knowledge and understanding of what God's Word teaches on this subject? How many marriages fail simply because husbands and wives know only how to live with one another according to the philosophies and manner of an unbelieving secular world? *Beware lest anyone cheat you through philosophy and empty deceit, according to the tradition of men, according to the basic principles of the world, and not according to Christ. (Colossians 2:8)*

The goal of this book is to equip all who read it to either prepare for a future marriage, or strengthen/save their current marriage. There is no reason to live in a marital relationship spiritually blind on this matter, and there is no reason to approach the wedding day with an underlying fear of failing one another down the road. We have been given all knowledge and understanding by a loving Father, if only we would humble ourselves and heed His teachings. *His divine power has given to us all things that pertain to life and godliness, through the knowledge of Him who called us... (2 Peter 1:3)*

Chapter Two

Biblical Foundations of Marriage

Today there is an extreme deviation between what the Bible teaches on marriage and what couples in modern society actually practice. Because of this, it is crucial to lay a foundation of biblical truths which address God's original purpose and intention concerning the institution of marriage. First, we need to understand the creation of male and female was intentional and purposeful. Male and female genders are not an evolutionary accident brought about by random chance and time. The Bible teaches us both genders were created by God, and expressly in the image of God. This means, just as God Himself is a trinity made up of the Father (soul), the Son (body) and the Holy Spirit (spirit) so too are men and women created as triune entities made up of body, soul and spirit. *So God created man in His own image; in the image of God He created him; male and female He created them. (Genesis 1:27)*

Secondly, the Bible teaches God instituted marriage and its resulting gift of procreation in order to solve the problem of human loneliness. *And the LORD God said, "It is not good that man should be alone; I will make him a helper comparable to him. Out of the ground the LORD God formed every beast of the field and every bird of the air, and brought them to Adam to see what he would call them. And whatever Adam called each living creature; that was its name. So Adam gave names to all cattle, to the birds of the air, and to every beast of the field. But for Adam there was not found a helper comparable to him. And the LORD God caused a deep sleep to fall on Adam, and he slept; and He took one of his ribs, and closed up the flesh in its place. Then the rib which the LORD God had taken from man He made into a woman, and He brought her to the man. (Genesis 2:18-22)*

Marriage will result in an inseparable bonding of "oneness" between the husband and wife which is meant to last the duration of their lifetime. *Therefore a man shall leave his father and mother and cleave to his wife, and they shall become one flesh. (Genesis 2:24)* The verb "cleave" is defined as 'to adhere to, cling to, follow close and hard after, be joined together, or stick to'. This word demonstrates unwavering loyalty and an active, pursuing, unconditional (agape) love that refuses to let go.

11

God intended for marriage to be a blessing not only on an emotional level but a physical one as well. Within the confines of the marriage relationship God commands Adam and Eve to be fruitful and multiply. This involves an intimate, physical union without shame. *And they were both naked, the man and his wife, and were not ashamed. (Genesis 2:25)* The Bible uses a Hebrew verb which in English translates into "knew" or "to know" in order to express this sexual union. *Now Adam knew Eve his wife, and she conceived and bore Cain, and said, "I have acquired a man from the LORD." (Genesis 4:1)* The word implies dignity, intimacy, and a tender, very personal and sacred knowledge of one another which no one else may participate in or share.

The definition of the word "holy" is "to be set apart, worthy of veneration, sacred". A wife is deemed holy or "set apart" for only her husband, and a husband is deemed holy or "set apart" for only his wife. Sex within marriage is a beautiful, creative gift given to a husband and wife from our generous and creative God, and He deems it honorable, undefiled and holy. *Marriage is honorable among all, and the bed undefiled; but fornicators and adulterers God will judge. (Hebrews 13:4)* The physical union in marriage which results in procreation is also a beautiful picture which mirrors the three-fold image of God, creating a husband-wife-child trinity while glorifying His creative nature.

So then, they are no longer two but one flesh. Therefore what God has joined together, let not man separate. (Matthew 19:6) (Mark 10:9) In these passages, God makes it very clear that while the choice to get married may be in the hands of men and women, once the oaths happen and the physical union takes place, God is the authority Who joins them or "yokes" them together, changing the two into "one". Because it is He Who performs this special joining, God instructs that no man should ever attempt to separate such a union. Essentially the Bible tells us the physical union between husband and wife results in an unseen bond created by God Himself. It is also important to note, the two become "one" regardless of whether or not the choice of spouse was the best one for those people. If consummated and lived out in a biblical, agape love fashion according to God's teachings, the marriage will be a success and a blessing, and it will last a lifetime.

Physical intimacy between a husband and wife can be viewed as the spiritual "superglue" meant to fuse a couple strongly together in unity for all times; through periods of great blessing as well as periods of great tribulation. And because it is a holy act causing two people to be cleaved to one another spiritually, it is a very damaging thing to commit that same act with anyone else. Like two fingers super-glued together and then forced apart, causing injury to the skin on both fingers; the separating of two people who have physically cleaved to one another in sexual union will also cause lasting damage to both partners, emotionally and spiritually. This is the reason why adultery and sex outside of marriage are so destructive.

Sexual promiscuity destroys the picture and pattern of God's image, His purpose for the marital union, and it also tears apart the spiritual bond created between men and women when they have sex with one another. In addition to many negative physical consequences, the spiritual and emotional scarring which takes place when one leads a life practicing sex outside of marriage increasingly harms one's ability to healthily and successfully cleave to one single person in the union of marriage down the road.

God intended for men and women to find a marriage partner while young and in their physical and sexual prime. This biblical principle directly opposes the self-focused, materialism oriented ideals of today's secular world which persuade young men and women to wait until they are older before they get married. Today's couples are told it is better to get an education, establish a career, buy a house, and become financially stable *before* pursuing marriage. By these standards, a typical person won't be ready to get married until they are in their 30's or even 40's! There is no logic to this. Biblically and biologically, such a game plan makes no sense. How can a person be expected to stay sexually pure for such a long time and specifically during the very best years of his or her young life?

The "wait-until-you're-older" strategy either results in the most attractive and most hormonally active years of one's young adult life engaging in uncommitted, damaging and sinful sexual promiscuity, or conversely, a senseless period of forced celibacy during one's prime of life as he or she awaits the "acceptable time" to get married. Neither path is sensible, natural, or tolerable. God certainly did not intend for young adults to remain single and vulnerable to loneliness and sexual temptation for such a long period of time. He created the institution of marriage specifically to solve such a problem.

The devil, on the other hand, loves to promote sexual immorality and encourage the inherent original sin of human selfishness and self-love. As such, he has been very successful in bringing our culture to a point where our television shows, movies, advertisements, music, education system, and even political arena all strongly promote the understanding that people should spend their young adult lives living for themselves, indulging in any and every experience they desire. The consequence of such a path is the creation of a society filled with people who have developed such deeply engrained, self-focused, self-gratifying habits of living that even if they do decide to get married in their 30's or later they can hardly be fit for the role. The ability to truly commit to one relationship for a lifetime becomes dysfunctional and damaged, and the capacity for learning to put another's needs first or live for anyone but self is greatly diminished.

God's intended path for men and women is so much better. It is clearly during those very young adulthood years that one should be developing a committed, youthful love relationship and enjoying an active sex life with a spouse. God instituted marriage so young husbands and wives could face life on earth together in unity and marital fellowship as they learn the ways of adulthood, responsibility, and parenting. It is through the bonding of shared challenges, shared hardships, and shared blessings that young married couples naturally grow their relationships closer and stronger.

Realistically, it is far easier to learn to share one's time, space, energy, and self when one is young. It is far easier to learn to be giving, affectionate, and attentive to one another's needs when one is young. It is far easier to enjoy a healthy and exciting marital sex life when one is young and attractive. It is far easier to get pregnant, be pregnant, and give birth when one is young. It is far easier to have the vitality and patience for parenting when one is young. Biblically, God shows us by example and by His commands that His intent was for men and women to make the lifelong commitment to marriage when they are still young. *Let your fountain be blessed, and rejoice with the wife of your youth. (Proverbs 5:18)* The primary purpose for marriage is to dispel human loneliness and to avoid the temptation of sexual sin. *...but if they cannot exercise self-control, let them marry. For it is* *better to marry than to burn with passion. (1ˢᵗ Corinthians 7:9)*

God intended the marriage union to glorify Him and His creative, triune nature. His best plan for us involves our cleaving and committing to only one partner in the holy sanctity of marriage while we are young and therefore sexually undefiled. Because it is God's best plan for the human race, we find the institution of marriage continually under a demonic, spiritually motivated attack via politics, public education, media and music, and the ever-increasing degradation of societal norms and morals. The devil cannot hurt God, so he instead works diligently to hurt God's image-bearers; the human race.

The godless, self-seeking individuality promoted by today's culture is one of the primary contributing factors in unhealthy marriage relationships and is simply an expression of mankind's original sin. Husbands and wives are all too often involved in serving "self" over serving one another. This is the choice Adam and Eve made in the Garden of Eden and it is the same attitude encouraged in society today. When such a worldview is combined with the stunning lack of understanding regarding what biblically ordained marital love or "agape" love is and looks like on a practical basis, it is no wonder we are overwhelmed with divorces, damaged and struggling relationships, and couples choosing to make no commitments to one another whatsoever. Believers and unbelievers alike have allowed a pervasive preoccupation with self to infiltrate every aspect of daily life. This results in relationally-destructive behavior patterns and shallow, unfulfilling partnerships fettered with resentment, emotional upset, and distrust. Such things are not what God intended for us.

Chapter Three

The Marital Role of Wives

Another issue affecting marriage today is the fact that husbands and wives tend to take on unbiblical roles within the marital relationship. Let us first examine the role of wives. Modern wives – believers and unbelievers alike – often find themselves trying to either lead the marriage relationship or co-lead alongside their husbands. This is due to an overcorrecting, ultra-feminist idealism which has become embedded into our culture, and as such it is single-handedly destroying God's intended marital harmony. We have reached a point where men are no longer taught to be strong, responsible, masculine leaders but instead they are emasculated from boyhood and onward, socially pressured to be apathetic, weak, passive and compromising versions of their intended nature. Conversely, women are now taught to assume aggressive and often relationally dominant roles in society and within their own marriages; roles which do not fit their God-purposed nature no matter how hard they try.

This upside-down behavior results in upside-down marriages. Today we commonly see scenarios in which the husband appears to exhibit the conduct of the "biggest child" in the household as he is routinely corrected, reprimanded, and dominated by the wife; or in other cases, we see marriages which can truly be defined as the proverbial "two-headed monster" where both spouses battle one another to be in charge, naturally causing friction and disharmony. Either type of marital relationship is doomed for failure because neither spouse is fulfilling the roles God intended for them to fill.

What does the Bible say about the marriage role of the wife? First, let's remind ourselves what we found in Genesis on this topic: *And the LORD God said, "It is not good that man should be alone; I will make him a helper comparable to him. Out of the ground the LORD God formed every beast of the field and every bird of the air, and brought them to Adam to see what he would call them. And whatever Adam called each living creature; that was its name. So Adam gave names to all cattle, to the birds of the air, and to every beast of the field. But for Adam there was not found a helper comparable to him. And the LORD God caused a deep sleep to fall on Adam, and he slept; and*

He took one of his ribs, and closed up the flesh in its place. Then the rib which the LORD God had taken from man He made into a woman, and He brought her to the man. (Genesis 2:18-22)

We can see from this section of Scripture that the wife is designed by God to be the husband's helper. The term "helper" refers to a beneficial relationship where one person supports and aids the other as a friend, ally, support system, encourager, and backup. The Greek word in the original texts is "parakletos" or "paraclete" and is defined as "advocate or helper". The word is often used to describe the action and nature of the Holy Spirit in a believer's life. God's calling for the believing wife is to be the husband's advocate in all things. She is called by God to encourage her husband to thrive in his relationship with God, and in his roles as provider, protector, husband, father, and head of his home.

The role of the wife as "helper" is not a diminished or lowly role but in fact is a vital, dynamic, and extremely key role. As mentioned before, "Helper" is a title given to the Holy Spirit, *But the Helper, the Holy Spirit, whom the Father will send in My name, He will teach you all things, and bring to your remembrance all things that I said to you. (John 14:26)* and it is also a title which God takes on for Himself when He tells us He is our Help [Helper] in times of need or trouble. *God is our refuge and strength, a very present help in trouble. (Psalm 46:1)* This role is Spirit-led and actively functions upon the foundation of the wife's agape love toward her husband as well as her personal obedience to God.

Therefore, wives, please understand; no matter the situation, and no matter your mood, never forget that in your marriage God has given you a holy calling to be a helper, encourager, and advocate for your husband. You are called to help your husband be the very best man of God he can be, you are to help him keep Jesus in front of his eyes at all times, you are to help him grow in the Lord, and you are to help him juggle work, kids, and daily life while he bears the God-instructed burden of being the head of your home. You are to help him feel loved, admired, valued, and confident. You are to help him feel respected, depended upon, needed, desired, and important to you. The role of a wife is one of the most crucial, integral callings a woman can have and is a far weightier matter than most people realize. God has called wives to be the backbone and support of their husbands. A wife must stand securely, faithfully, and trustingly behind her husband as he forges his way through life in this broken and corrupt world. When a woman chooses to become married her career becomes secondary, her hobbies become secondary, and her goals must change – both long term and daily. It is an honor, and a gift, and a godly calling, to become a helpmate to a godly husband.

Unfortunately in our society most women do not see their roles in this light. They do not see themselves as having such a vital responsibility. They do not view everyday situations through the lens of the Holy Spirit on this matter and many are missing their precious opportunities to regularly encourage and lift their husbands up or simply make it a joy for him to come home after a long day's work. Instead, women have a natural propensity to nag, vent, or complain the moment their husbands walk through the door. Many wives will also fall into a pattern of arguing or displaying scorn and impatience with their husbands as a regular part of marital communication. This innate propensity to be contentious is the direct result of the curse found in Genesis 3. *To the woman He said: "I will greatly multiply your sorrow and your conception; in pain you shall bring forth children; your desire shall be for your husband, and he shall rule over you."* *(Genesis 3:16)* Because Eve heeded the devil and disobeyed God's instructions, leading Adam into eating the forbidden fruit after she first ate of it herself, God declared childbearing will become painful for all women, and He also avowed that a woman's sin nature will cause her to have a [wrong] desire to lead or rule over her husband, just as Eve took it upon herself to do so in the garden of Eden. Our English translation of this passage is a bit lacking, but we do have a parallel passage in Genesis 4:7 in which God is speaking to Cain about his anger at his offering not being acceptable; *"If you do well, will you not be accepted? And if you do not do well, sin lies at the door. And its desire is for you, but you should rule over it."* *(Genesis 4:7)* The grammar used in the original Hebrew here is the same as what we find in Genesis 3:16. The Bible is showing us a warning about sin personified and how its desire is to rule over man, but man should choose to rule over it. This is how we can better understand Eve's curse from Genesis 3:16. She will have an innate desire to rule over her man, but her man must instead rule over her for the marriage relationship to be in harmony. Therefore, we now have a biblical understanding why so many wives are inherently quick to become

25

critical of their husband's behavior and choices. It is a curse and a direct result of Eve wrongly taking a leadership role back in the Garden of Eden. Women who do not hold this propensity in check will live out their marriages habitually seeking to rule over their husbands with their own specific demands, rules, and corrections.

Such behavior is incredibly destructive to the marriage relationship and quickly chips away at the headship, confidence, and authority a husband must have in his own home. *A continual dripping on a very rainy day and a contentious woman are alike. (Proverbs 27:15)* Wives must learn to guard their hearts against such behavior. *Better to dwell in a corner of a housetop than in a house shared with a contentious woman. (Proverbs 21:12)* We must grasp the understanding that ceaseless nagging, criticism, and complaints do not change a man's unwanted behavior. Only God can correct a man from within should he require it, and He is able to do this much more quickly if the husband has a faithful, loving, praying wife who exhibits a quiet and gentle spirit as she trusts in God for the marriage relationship. *Wives, likewise, be submissive to your own husbands, that even if some do not obey the word, they, without a word, may be won by the conduct of their wives, when they observe your chaste conduct accompanied by fear [reverence/respect]. Do not let your adornment be merely outward — arranging the hair, wearing gold, or putting on fine apparel — rather let it be the hidden person of the heart, with the incorruptible beauty of a gentle and quiet spirit, which is very precious in the sight of God. For in this manner, in former times, the holy women who trusted in God also adorned themselves, being submissive to their own husbands, as Sarah obeyed Abraham... (1 Peter 3:1-6)*

The passage above indicates that the wife must seek to nurture a gentle and quiet spirit within herself. The Bible says this is *very precious to God* – Wow! That factor alone should be more than enough to motivate believing wives to continually discipline their tongues and tempers. The biblically-minded wife realizes she is not meant to be the authority figure in the marriage relationship. She understands she wouldn't want such a role for it would create a domineering behavior within her that is completely unattractive to the husband, and would emasculate the husband in such a way that he becomes completely unattractive to her as well. The understanding is simple. Much of marital disharmony and conflict can be linked to the fall of mankind, the curse, and the mixed-up relationship roles which original sin created.

Therefore, it is extremely crucial for wives to fulfill their original, God-given roles within the parameters of the marriage relationship. *Wives, submit to your own husbands, as is fitting in the Lord. (Colossians 3:18)* The role of the wife is equally valuable but different than that of the husband. It is complementary to the husband, yet equally dignified. The point being, while God values both husband and wife equally, there is an order and a hierarchy when it comes to position. *But I want you to know that the head of every man is Christ, the head of woman is man, and the head of Christ is God. (1 Corinthians 11:3)* God calls the husband to be the head of the marriage relationship. *Wives, submit to your own husbands, as to the Lord. For the husband is head of the wife, as also Christ is head of the church; and He is the Savior of the body. Therefore, just as the church is subject to Christ, so let the wives be to their own husbands in everything. (Ephesians 5:22-24)*

An interesting verse in the Book of Titus discusses the role of older women teaching younger women how to behave in their marriages. *...the older women likewise, that they be reverent in behavior, not slanderers, not given to much wine, teachers of good things - that they admonish the young women to love their husbands, to love their children, to be discreet, chaste, homemakers, good, obedient to their own husbands,*

28

that the word of God may not be blasphemed. (Titus 2:3-5) Notice the reason we are given as to why women should be taught the behaviors listed above - that the word of God may not be blasphemed. It is so important to realize our behavior as believers, whether it is within our God-given marital roles or elsewhere, must always be looked at in light of our witness to the world as ambassadors of Jesus Christ. We must continually strive to shine the light of Jesus in our own particular spheres of influence. We are directed to glorify God in how we speak and in how we act so He is not blasphemed. *And whatever you do in word or deed, do all in the name of the Lord Jesus, giving thanks to God the Father through Him. (Colossians 3:17)* A wife who proclaims to the world she is a Christian woman does great harm to God's name and His word if she is not living a life of loving, helpful, and joyous servanthood toward her husband.

Who can find a virtuous wife?
For her worth is far above rubies.
The heart of her husband safely trusts her;
So he will have no lack of gain.
She does him good and not evil
All the days of her life.
She seeks wool and flax,
And willingly works with her hands
She is like the merchant ships,
She brings her food from afar.
She also rises while it is yet night,
And provides food for her household,
And a portion for her maidservants.
She considers a field and buys it;
From her profits she plants a vineyard.
She girds herself with strength,
And strengthens her arms.
She perceives that her merchandise is good,
And her lamp does not go out by night.
She stretches out her hands to the distaff,
And her hand holds the spindle.
She extends her hand to the poor,
Yes, she reaches out her hands to the needy.
She is not afraid of snow for her household,
For all her household is clothed with scarlet.
She makes tapestry for herself;
Her clothing is fine linen and purple.
Her husband is known in the gates,
When he sits among the elders of the land.
She makes linen garments and sells them,
And supplies sashes for the merchants.
Strength and honor are her clothing;
She shall rejoice in time to come.
She opens her mouth with wisdom,
And on her tongue is the law of kindness.

She watches over the ways of her household,
And does not eat the bread of idleness.
Her children rise up and call her blessed;
Her husband also, and he praises her:
"Many daughters have done well,
But you excel them all."
Charm is deceitful and beauty is passing,
But a woman who fears the LORD, she shall be praised.
Give her of the fruit of her hands,
And let her own works praise her in the gates.

– Proverbs 31

Chapter Four

The Marital Role of Husbands

Now let us examine what the Bible says about the role of the husband. Again, beginning with the Genesis verses, we can see something important about the creation of Adam and Eve and that is, Adam was created first. God formed the woman only after He created all other creatures and found none suitable as a helper and companion for the man. Eve was formed *from* Adam, *for* Adam, and then given *to* Adam; *And the LORD God caused a deep sleep to fall on Adam, and he slept; and He took one of his ribs and closed up the flesh in its place. Then the rib which the LORD God had taken from man He made into a woman, and He brought her to the man. And Adam said: "This is now bone of my bones and flesh of my flesh; She shall be called Woman, because she was taken out of Man." (Genesis 2:21-23)* A wife is truly a gift to a man from God. Because the first woman was created from the first man and formed into a separate being, the picture created by marriage is one of completion – the two shall become one, making both partners whole.

Therefore a man shall leave his father and mother and cleave to his wife, and they shall become one flesh. (Genesis 2:24) So then, they are no longer two but one flesh. Therefore what God has joined together, let not man separate. (Matthew 19:6) (Mark 10:9)

How is a man supposed to treat such a wonderful gift from his Creator? Well our Lord says the husband is to cherish his wife; honoring her and treating her as though she were a precious, priceless vase; something delicate and beautiful; a gift not to be taken for granted. Husbands are also directed to be understanding of the wife and her needs, which requires a spiritual leading and purposeful spiritual obedience to be patient and kind with her at all times. *Husbands, likewise, dwell with them with understanding, giving honor to the wife, as to the weaker [fragile, precious] vessel, and as being heirs together of the grace of life, that your prayers may not be hindered. (1 Peter 3:7)* In this verse, husbands are commanded to practice understanding and honor toward their wives, which indicates this is not something that comes naturally but rather something which must be willfully and purposefully learned. *Husbands, love your wives and do not be bitter toward them. (Colossians 3:19)* From the above verse we can deduce husbands may have a tendency to feel bitter or hostile toward the wife - most likely when she is being contentious or disrespectful! Notice the commands we have from God are always against those sinful things which we have a natural tendency to do if we are not allowing the Holy Spirit to lead us. So, here we see God commanding husbands to practice agape love toward their wives regardless of any innate flesh reactions to feel bitter as a result of a wife's personal needs or wrong behavior. This requires Spirit-led prompting which will spring forth from a man's willful obedience to God.

It is interesting to note from the 1 Peter 3:7 passage there is a consequence for husbands who do not seek to live with their wives in the manner in which God commands. Husbands who are not being obedient on this issue will have their prayers hindered. The definition of "hinder" is to "create difficulties resulting in delay or obstruction", and secondarily, "to impede, thwart, halt, interfere with, hold back or hold up". What a serious thing it is to have one's prayers hindered and therefore, what a frightening warning!

Additionally, the Bible makes it very clear husbands are to love their wives sacrificially just as Jesus loves His bride, the church, sacrificially. *Husbands, love your wives, just as Christ also loved the church and gave Himself for her, that He might sanctify and cleanse her with the washing of water by the word, that He might present her to Himself a glorious church, not having spot or wrinkle or any such thing, but that she should be holy and without blemish. So husbands ought to love their own wives as their own bodies; he who loves his wife loves himself. For no one ever hated his own flesh, but nourishes and cherishes it, just as the Lord does the church. (Ephesians 5:25-29* Just as wives must be commanded by God to respect and submit to their husbands because it doesn't come naturally, so must husbands be commanded by God to sacrificially love their wives, as his sin nature gives him a propensity not to show her such a compassionate "agape" love and self-sacrifice on a daily basis. The Ephesians 5 passages also show us in more detail what the husband is commanded to fulfill in terms of caring for his wife. He is not only called to sacrificially love her, putting her needs ahead of his own, but he is also responsible for the spiritual leadership in their relationship. He is tasked with building her up in the knowledge of the Word of God and strengthening her fellowship with Christ by *sanctifying and cleansing her with the washing of water by the word.* Obviously, this involves studying Scripture together, worshipping together, praying

35

together, being obedient to the Lord together, and regularly gathering with other believers together.

In all of these things, it is the sacrificial, life-giving love of God which a husband is to be imitating and practicing toward his wife. *By this we know love, because He laid down His life for us. And we also ought to lay down our lives for the brethren. (1 John 3:16)* The husband must love his wife the way Jesus loves the church; unconditionally, faithfully, changelessly, and regardless of her response. *In this the love of God was manifested toward us, that God has sent His only begotten Son into the world, that we might live through Him. In this is love, not that we loved God, but that He loved us and sent His Son to be the propitiation for our sins. Beloved, if God so loved us, we also ought to love one another. (1 John 4:9-11)* Again, this is agape love in action. It is a love that acts first: *We love Him because He first loved us (1 John 4:19)* It is a love given for the benefit of the receiver; an edifying, caring, compassionate, life-giving, selfless, providing and protecting kind of love. *Nevertheless let each one of you in particular so love his own wife as himself, and let the wife see that she respects her husband. (Ephesians 5:33)* When the marriage relationship is viewed from the lens of

Scripture, and the husband and wife are understood to have become "One", it becomes a very simple thing for a husband to realize he is now empowered to treat his wife as well as he treats himself. *For no one ever hated his own flesh, but nourishes and cherishes it, just as the Lord does the church. (Ephesians 5:29)* It also becomes evident that when a husband begins to practice such a profound, sacrificial, and unconditional love towards his wife, she cannot help but thrive on every level and as a result will naturally submit to him and respect him the way she has been commanded.

Finally, as we already determined when viewing the biblical role of the wife in marriage, God's calling for the husband is one of leadership, authority and responsibility. *But I want you to know that the head of every man is Christ, the head of woman is man, and the head of Christ is God. (1 Corinthians 11:3)* The ultimate responsibility for the well-being of the wife is laid at the husband's feet. He is her head, he is her provider, he is her authority and he is responsible for making sure her needs are met physically, emotionally, intellectually, and spiritually. We have a complicated verse in 1 Corinthians which speaks of the spiritual headship a husband has over his wife, and in essence, it is a passage which explains the husband's headship or "covering" is necessary for the spiritual protection of the wife. *For a man indeed ought not to cover his head, since he is the image and glory of God; but woman is the glory of man. For man is not from woman, but woman from man. Nor was man created for the woman, but woman for the man. For this reason the woman ought to have a symbol of authority on her head, because of the angels. Nevertheless, neither is man independent of woman, nor woman independent of man, in the Lord. For as woman came from man, even so man also comes through woman; but all things are from God. (1 Corinthians 11:7-12)*

As we saw with Eve in Genesis, God appears to have created women with what some people like to describe as "extra-long spiritual antennae" in the sense that women tend to be more easily tuned-in to the spiritual realm than men. Essentially, it is often women who will "hear from the Lord" or notice a spiritual prompting on an issue long before a man does. Women tend to be more spiritually receptive and respond to God's call of repentance and salvation through Jesus Christ more quickly than most men. However, there is a warning regarding the heightened spiritual awareness of women which we must heed. As in Eve's case, women can be too quick to act on spiritual promptings without taking the time to discern whether they are hearing godly truth versus a deceiving evil spirit. Therefore, we have the 1 Corinthians passage above as well as the 1 Timothy passage below which both indicate the husband has authority over the wife not only because he was created before her and she was created for him, but secondarily, his authority and headship are for her own spiritual protection since she is more apt to be spiritually led astray by fallen angels (demons) or by the devil himself. *Let a woman learn in silence with all submission. And I do not permit a woman to teach or to have authority over a man, but to be in silence. For Adam was formed first, then Eve. And Adam was not deceived, but the woman being deceived, fell into transgression. (1 Timothy 2:11-14)*

Chapter Five

The Biblical Prescription for Marriage

What does a healthy marriage look like? The answer to this question has everything to do with what agape love looks like in action. Remember, we have learned agape love is an unconditional, sacrificial, servanthood love borne out of will and purpose. Our first example of what agape love looks like is found within the actions of God Himself. The Bible teaches us God is [agape] love. *And we have known and believed the love that God has for us. God is love, and he who abides in love abides in God, and God in him. (1 John 4:16)* God loves us unconditionally though we do not deserve His love. He treats us with His unmerited favor, grace and mercy regardless of our own words, attitudes and behavior. He loves us sacrificially through His Son, Jesus Christ, Who died on the cross to atone for the spiritual rebellion and self-led sinful nature of the entire world; past, present and future. *For God so loved the world that*

He gave His only begotten Son, that whoever believes in Him should not perish but have everlasting life. (John 3:16) God sacrificed His Only Son even for those who hate and revile Him as an enemy. *But God demonstrates his own love for us in this: While we were still sinners, Christ died for us...For if, while we were God's enemies, we were reconciled to him through the death of his Son, how much more, having been reconciled, shall we be saved through his life!* (Romans 5:8-10) God loves us in deed and in truth; and He encourages us to love others in the same manner. *My little children, let us not love in word or in tongue, but in deed and in truth.* (1 John 3:18) God's love for us does not falter based on a bad day or an ugly situation. He is faithful even when we are not. God's agape love for us and the resulting actions of that love do not ever change; His mercies toward us are new every morning. *Through the LORD's mercies we are not consumed, because His compassions fail not. They are new every morning; great is Your faithfulness.* (Lamentations 3:22, 23) His love is everlasting, and given to us purely out of His choice and His will for our benefit, for our blessing, and for our good. That is agape love. This kind of love is only possible because God's love is not founded in the flesh but rather in the Spirit, as He is Spirit. *God is Spirit, and those who worship Him must worship in spirit and truth.* (John 4:24)

Therefore, just like God's love for us, the true love (agape love) between a husband and wife is also supposed to consist of an active choice of the will and continual, purposeful, beneficial action toward one another. Loving one's spouse is not merely about experiencing a strong emotion. True love is not just a passionate, erotic feeling that makes your heart beat fast and puts butterflies in your stomach when you are together. The Bible actually teaches us our heartfelt emotions and feelings cannot be trusted. *The heart is deceitful above all things, and desperately wicked; who can know it? (Jeremiah 17:9)* The point being, passionate feelings and exciting emotions will fade with time and comfortable familiarity; but the unconditional, choice-based, agape love of God does not. The agape love of God is a selfless love and it is this very same unconditional, never-ending, servanthood love a marriage requires in order to be fruitful and harmonious. Agape love calls for loving words and loving behavior even when one's spouse isn't acting very nice. This is a love that puts the needs and feelings of your spouse ahead of your own – without complaint, without resentment, and without fail. It is a love that desires the best for the beloved no matter the cost to self.

Can you imagine a marriage relationship in which both partners seek to practice such a selfless love toward one another? Agape love *is* the kind of love the Bible speaks of with regard to husbands and wives. It is a love not dependent upon feelings, sexual chemistry, or an anticipated reciprocal response. True agape love seeks to exhibit intentional good will toward the beloved no matter the mood, situation, or tedium of daily living in a fallen world. In essence, this level of love requires a personal commitment to do what is in the best interests of one's spouse in every moment. Agape love is part of the wedding day oath most people make at the altar, to "love one another in good times and bad, in sickness and health..." and as such it involves dying to oneself daily for the sake of our partner's happiness, health, well-being, and encouragement. It is a love which involves learning to rise above bad moods, laziness, hurt feelings, or exasperation in order to treat one's spouse lovingly and peaceably no matter the situation. The giving of this level of love will eventually produce the same type of love behavior in the recipient as well as increase the feelings of love in both partners.

Historically, many culturally mandated marriage arrangement practices were often very successful because people in such cultures understood the concept of agape love and actively practiced it. When both partners demonstrate such behavior toward one another, a feeling-based love simply grows – even between two strangers who did not choose one another. Agape love appears incredibly costly to self on the surface but when one works to foster such a love through practice and patience, it will result in great marital blessings and earthly joy with one's spouse.

This kind of love sounds like it would be virtually impossible for any human being to practice, but let me assure you it is something a believer absolutely can learn to do, and in fact, it is something believers are *commanded* to do throughout Scripture. Because agape love is a Spirit-led love, it is something the secular world cannot truly understand. Nonbelievers are not equipped to love anyone completely in this manner because being able to do so requires an understanding of who Jesus Christ is and what He has done on the cross. It also requires the leading and empowerment of the Holy Spirit which is given only to believers by God. As believers, if we equip ourselves with knowledge about this subject from God's Word and allow the Holy Spirit to lead us in such behavior toward our spouse, we will find ourselves thriving in a marriage filled with peace, joy, sexual satisfaction, security, trust, and a sense of belonging. All other forms and expressions of love within the marriage will become fruitful and healthy when agape love is practiced as a foundation. Practically speaking, Husbands and wives can display agape love in their marriages by working to be a blessing to their partners in every way possible on a daily basis. With both words and behavior they must seek to edify, strengthen, admire, and be complimentary toward each other. There should never be anything spoken that tears down, blames or criticizes. Spouses must spend time with one another valuing each other's company and enjoying conversation, experiences, feelings and physical affection regularly.

Agape love is both the preventive medicine that protects against marital failure and the cure for even severely damaged relationships. This is the love God has for us and if we want to be blessed and at peace in our marriages we must strive to practice it toward our spouses on a daily basis.

When one lives a life giving unconditional love to their spouse, they will find there is no tumultuous, emotionally upset, uncontrolled *reaction* to the negative situations that will inevitably pop up. Instead there will simply be spirit-led, self-controlled, faithful, peaceful, humbled, uncomplaining, and consistently loving *action* toward one another. *And above all things have fervent love for one another, for love will cover a multitude of sins. Be hospitable to one another without grumbling. (1 Peter 4:8, 9)* We must embrace God's definition of agape love, memorizing it and embedding it into our hearts so we can strive to practice it toward others, especially our spouses, on a daily basis: *Love suffers long and is kind; love does not envy; love does not parade itself, is not puffed up; does not behave rudely, does not seek its own, is not provoked, thinks no evil; does not rejoice in iniquity, but rejoices in the truth; bears all things, believes all things, hopes all things, endures all things. Love never fails. (1 Corinthians 13:4-8)*

These words are not meaningless platitudes created simply to be recited during wedding ceremonies. God means for husbands and wives to learn such teachings and take them deeply to heart in order to actively live them out with one another.

Chapter Six

Biblical Principles of Intimacy

Therefore a man shall leave his father and mother and be joined to his wife, and they shall become one flesh. (Genesis 2:24) When couples first fall in love, they tend to spend all their free time together eating meals, attending gatherings and social functions, going to coffee shops, music concerts and sports events, ice skating, hiking, bicycling, golfing, watching movies, having picnics, etc.... They cannot help but want to spend every spare moment together. This is how couples develop an intimately familiar relationship with one another. The more time spent together, the more a couple will build common experiences and common bonds which ultimately results in the wonderful closeness needed for a strong marriage. Intimacy is a key part of every healthy marriage relationship and it begins to grow simply by spending a great deal of time with one another. The ultimate expression of a couple's intimacy is fulfilled within the physical union between man and wife which God declares makes them "one flesh".

However, after the excitement of the dating and honeymoon phase begins to fade and the daily routines of married life become more settled, sometimes couples have a tendency to fall back into pursuing those things they individually did before they met one another. This change eventually causes a form of separation in the marriage relationship and works to destroy those intimate 'togetherness' bonds initially experienced. For example, in today's social culture many husbands get together with business colleagues, neighbors, male relatives or school buddies in order to spend time socializing together without their wives, whether it is golfing, hunting, fishing, playing cards or hitting a local sports bar to watch a game. Conversely, married women will find themselves participating in "girls' night out" events or getting together with coworkers, female relatives or girlfriends to go antiquing, mall shopping, attend craft fairs or book club gatherings. In either case, there is certainly nothing wrong with this kind of thing if it is done only once awhile or doesn't consume too much of a couple's leisure time on a regular basis. All too often though, such pursuits become a frequent habit and lead to spouses functioning like the two separate people they were before they got married, which is very detrimental to God's concept of marital "oneness".

Husbands and wives simply should not be routinely enjoying a lot of leisure time apart. *Do life together.* Learn to enjoy what your spouse enjoys, and ask your spouse to be involved with the things you enjoy doing. Again, in God's eyes, a married couple is now one person. *So then, they are no longer two but one flesh. Therefore what God has joined together, let not man separate. (Matthew 19:6)* Spouses who habitually choose to pursue activities that don't involve each other will eventually begin to lose their sense of intimacy with one another. Additionally, being without each other's company in such a manner can expose either one of them to wrong or questionable situations which may lead to suspicion and lack of trust in the marriage. Hand in hand with this is the understanding that spouses cannot continue to pursue singular friendships with those of the opposite gender. For example, if a wife has a close friend who is a man, she no longer may send him chatty texts or meet him for lunch or coffee by herself, no matter how harmless she may think it is. Obviously the same standard applies to the husband and any women he may have held friendships with prior to the marriage. The point is this...married men and women must never put themselves in a situation where one of them is socializing alone with a member of the opposite sex. Such behavior can lead to doubt, emotional separation, unsavory rumors and marital distress, not to mention extramarital attraction and eventual temptation to commit adultery.

A major part of marital intimacy and oneness involves the sexual relationship between the husband and wife. Don't ever let anyone persuade you sexual intimacy and chemistry isn't important or necessary for a healthy marriage. God deemed it so important He gives specific details as to how husbands and wives are to enjoy their physical relationship. *Let the husband render to his wife the affection due her, and likewise also the wife to her husband. The wife does not have authority over her own body, but the husband does. And likewise the husband does not have authority over his own body, but the wife does. Do not deprive one another except with consent for a time that you may give yourselves to fasting and prayer; and come together again so that Satan does not tempt you because of your lack of self-control..... (1 Corinthians 7:3-5)*

God not only created the institution of marriage for men and women to assuage human loneliness, He also created marriage to be the one place where human sexual desire and sexual pleasure can be enjoyed with His full approval and blessing. The passage below makes it clear God intends for sexual intimacy to be carried out solely within the confines of marriage ...*but if they [unmarried people] cannot exercise self-control, let them marry. For it is better to marry than to burn with passion. (1 Corinthians 7:9)* Sex is a monumentally important and uniting gift which God has given to husbands and wives. As was previously covered, sexual intimacy spiritually cleaves a couple to one another and can be viewed as the glue which binds the marriage relationship in a way like no other thing can. Sexual intimacy strips away all that stands between a husband and wife, bringing about a significant level of vulnerability, unity, and dependence upon one another.

That being said, look at the above verses again and notice what God is saying about physical intimacy. The passages clearly state the reason to marry is to be able to enjoy sex in a righteous and holy manner. God is literally saying those who burn with sexual passion should find a partner and marry them. The assumption then is that within the marriage the spouses are to enjoy sexual intimacy with one another often so they do not burn with passion, and so the devil cannot tempt them into sexual sin. The passages also indicate, once married, neither spouse may deprive the other of sexual activity unless both agree to do so for a short time and even then, only for the purpose of fasting and praying.

The lack of a healthy sex life between husbands and wives today is the number one reason for adultery and failed marriages. It seems to be a common curse in our society that after a year or two of marriage, or perhaps after the first or second baby is born, somehow sex becomes unimportant and even distasteful to the wife. She begins doling sexual experiences out like rare treats to an exasperated, frustrated husband. How does this happen? The answer to this question all too often brings us back to the subjects of agape love and biblically correct marriage roles between husbands and wives. There is a vicious cycle which starts in the home because the world does not know what agape love is and because husbands and wives no longer seek to fulfill biblically correct marital roles. Godly marriages are few and far between and as a result, the correct wisdom, knowledge, and understanding of what a godly marriage relationship should look like on a practical, daily basis, is nonexistent.

The following is an example of a typical, unhealthy marriage "vicious cycle scenario": A husband comes home and wants to relax in front of the television after a busy workday. A wife comes home from her own stressful day of work or else has been home with an endless list of housework and a demanding baby and toddler. Whatever the case, both spouses are tired from the day's responsibilities. Yet the dishwasher needs to be emptied, the garbage needs to be taken out, the dog needs to be walked, and whose turn is it to make dinner and/or change the next dirty diaper? As the husband attempts to relax in his favorite chair, the wife becomes exasperated and loses her temper. She naturally begins nagging or complaining [exhibiting her sin nature propensity to rule over him]. The more she complains, the more he ignores her and refuses to respond to her demands [exhibiting his sin nature tendency to purposefully withhold love and understanding toward her]. The result is a wife who is not practicing submissive, respectful behavior toward her husband and a husband who is not providing love, leadership, and understanding toward his wife.

Do you know what is difficult to do when you don't respect your husband? It's difficult to desire him and submit to him sexually. Therefore the wife stops wanting sexual intimacy with the husband and begins regularly rejecting his advances. The husband becomes hurt and frustrated by the routine rejection and withholds his love and attention from her even more. And the vicious cycle has begun. Sex has now become weaponized in the marriage and so has love. A wife who withholds her respect and submission in such a manner will eventually lead her husband to commit adultery with another woman. It does not matter how godly a man may be, if he is not receiving the warmth, admiration, respect and intimacy from his wife which his nature craves, somebody will come along and offer it to him one day and he will not be able to withstand the temptation. As one husband said to his estranged wife, "If I can't have sex with you, then who can I have it with?" It is a valid question. Conversely, a husband who continually withholds love, understanding and leadership from his wife will cause her to eventually commit adultery because she will one day stumble across a man who gives her the warmth, attention, understanding, and strong leadership she craves and she will not be able to withstand the temptation as well.

Chapter Seven

Spirit Led vs. Flesh Driven

We have established that God commands husbands and wives to faithfully practice an abiding and committed "agape" love toward one another. We have defined agape love as a purposeful, selfless, Spirit-led love and not simply a romantic feeling; more specifically, it is a choice-based love which values, serves, and gives unconditionally regardless of response. Now we must examine what the practical aspects of such a love look like on a daily basis. It is within this context the study of Spirit-led behavior versus flesh-driven behavior becomes imperative. First, what does the Bible teach about Spirit-led behavior? Galatians 5:22-25 states, *"But the fruit of the Spirit is love, joy, peace, longsuffering [patience], kindness, goodness, faithfulness, gentleness, self-control. Against such there is no law. And those who are Christ's have crucified the flesh with its passions and desires. If we live in the Spirit, let us also walk in the Spirit."*

This teaching is expanded on in Ephesians: *For you were once darkness, but now you are light in the Lord. Walk as children of light (for the fruit of the Spirit is in all goodness, righteousness, and truth), finding out what is acceptable to the Lord. (Ephesians 5:8-10)* As we examine the passages above, please note there is nothing wrong with having a healthy passion or desire toward the object of one's love. However in the context of the Galatians verse, the passions and desires which must be "crucified" are those powerful, sin-nature feelings which spring forth from human selfishness, self-focused ambitions, discontent, pride, greed, covetousness, or lust; and as such, they are evil.

Spirit-led behavior springs forth from both the power and leading of the Holy Spirit as well as from one's purposeful obedience to the precepts of God. Spirit-led behavior is about striving to faithfully imitate Jesus Christ as much as it is within our ability to do so on a daily basis. The more we practice, the easier it becomes, and the more discerning we will be about how we should handle ourselves in every situation. The writer of Hebrews encourages believers to mature in their faith and spiritual knowledge by living it out; actively practicing and utilizing God's precepts and following His commands. In doing so, the Christian sharpens their senses and increases their discernment *...those who by reason of use have their senses exercised to discern both good and evil. (Hebrews 5:14)* "By reason of use" asserts the Christian must continually practice what is commanded – which clearly means doing so is not a natural or innate ability but something which must be learned and willfully applied regularly. "Having their senses exercised" emphasizes the idea that through active practice one will exercise their spiritual senses and build discernment regarding spiritual things. Instead of mindlessly indulging in our easily offended, flesh-driven, knee-jerk reactions and self-focused thought processes, Spirit-led behavior will lead us to purposely pause and work diligently to take every thought captive, filtering it through the teachings of Jesus Christ before speaking or acting upon it. *...casting down arguments and every high thing that exalts itself against the knowledge of God, bringing every thought into captivity to the obedience of Christ. (2 Corinthians 10:5)*

It sounds cliché but there truly is such a thing as a "What would Jesus do" principle found in the Bible. As believers, we are called to imitate Christ in all aspects of our lives and this obviously includes how we treat our spouses. *Therefore be imitators of God as dear children. And walk in love, as Christ also has loved us and given Himself for us, an offering and a sacrifice to God for a sweet-smelling aroma. (Ephesians 5:1, 2)* Agape love enables a life to be lived in a joyous pattern of selfless, personal sacrifice for the best interests of the spouse and in spiritual obedience to God. This Spirit-led love produces a steady kindness and gentleness in our behavior. We will purposely choose not to react to negative marital situations in anger or defensiveness, but instead we will seek to impart soft words, concern, and compassion for the wellbeing of the spouse in such moments. *A soft answer turns away wrath, but a harsh word stirs up anger. (Proverbs 15:1)* How many marital arguments could be avoided or quickly diffused if husbands and wives would simply humble themselves and work to practice such fruits of the Spirit in their conversation and behavior?

Spirit-led behavior is proactive and others-focused. Flesh-driven behavior is reactive and self-focused. Spirit-led behavior requires us to take our eyes off of ourselves and direct them onto Jesus, His commands, and with regard to marriage, onto the object of our love. Spirit-led behavior seeks to fulfill our spouse's needs and what is best for him or her to thrive spiritually, emotionally, and practically on a daily basis. Spirit-led behavior carries us into a consistent pattern of peaceable existence not easily influenced by emotions or circumstances. Spirit-led people are influenced by the power of the Holy Spirit and the purposeful choice to regularly behave in a manner consistent with God's commands.

Conversely, flesh-driven behavior originates from our self-loving sin nature and more specifically, our pride. Flesh-driven people are unstable in all their ways; easily angered, easily offended or hurt, easily stressed and emotionally tossed about by every undesirable situation. The flesh-driven manner of functioning creates a lifestyle pattern of strife, argument, discontent, and resentment – a miserable place to be, especially within the parameters of marriage.

As Christians, we no longer have to be in bondage to offended feelings or hurt pride. God says we are new creations when we become born again and therefore we have the power to choose not be ruled by pride or any other sin anymore. *Therefore, if anyone is in Christ, he is a new creation; old things have passed away; behold, all things have become new. (2*

Corinthians 5:17) We are empowered by the Holy Spirit and the Word of God to be humble and to resist sin and the devil. *...God resists the proud, but gives grace to the humble. Therefore submit to God. Resist the devil and he will flee from you. (James 4:6, 7)* We must consciously put off our old sin nature and put on our new, spirit-led nature every single day, just like clothing. *...put off, concerning your former conduct, the old man which grows corrupt according to the deceitful lusts, and be renewed in the spirit of your mind, and that you put on the new man which was created according to God, in true righteousness and holiness. (Ephesians 4:22-24)*

We need to grasp the understanding that pride is the sin nature demand of the heart which drives us to constantly focus on self and how things affect us. Pride is what causes us to pursue our own comforts, goals, desires and pleasures without giving any thought to the will of God or the best interests of others. Pride is about self-love and self-rule. It is the original sin of the human race which was first carried out in the Garden of Eden. Pride says, "I will do what I want, I will be my own god, and I will pursue my own paths". Pride also says things like, "How dare this happen to me?" or "I can't believe someone treated me in such a way?" and, "I will repay evil for evil".

On the other hand, the Christian who is attentive to the leading of the Holy Spirit and operating in faith and humility says, "I will serve the LORD, I will serve my spouse." The Spirit-led Christian also asks, "What is God teaching me by allowing this trial?", and "What would Jesus have me do in this moment?" As Christians, we can know that when our spouse says or does something which is upsetting or hurtful, we are fully equipped to trust God for the situation and continue behaving in a positive, humble, godly, peaceable, patient and loving manner toward our partner. *I, therefore, the prisoner of the Lord, beseech you to walk worthy of the calling with which you were called, with all lowliness [humility] and gentleness, with longsuffering, bearing with one another in love, endeavoring to keep the unity of the Spirit in the bond of peace. There is one body and one Spirit, just as you were called in one hope of your calling; one Lord, one faith, one baptism; one God and Father of all, who is above all, and through all, and in you all. But to each one of us grace was given according to the measure of Christ's gift. (Ephesians 4:1-7)*

This is about controlling our own behavior regardless of the behavior of others.

Control what you have control over and leave the rest to God. It's that simple. No matter what your spouse is behaving like in any given moment, God commands you to do *your* part and fulfill *your* commanded role as peacefully as possible and without grumbling or resentment in your heart. *Be hospitable to one another without grumbling. (1 Peter 4:9)* It is so crucial to stop focusing on the wrong things your spouse did or said, and instead focus on the right things *you* are supposed to be doing, no matter the situation.

The marriage relationship is a wonderful, servanthood relationship which should bring both partners great unity, joy, intimacy, and harmonious rapport. God commands us to act in humility toward one another, serving one another and not thinking more highly of ourselves than we ought. *I beseech you therefore, brethren, by the mercies of God, that you present your bodies a living sacrifice, holy, acceptable to God, which is your reasonable service. And do not be conformed to this world, but be transformed by the renewing of your mind, that you may prove what is that good and acceptable and perfect will of God. For I say, through the grace given to me, to everyone who is among you, not to think of himself more highly than he ought to think, but to*

think soberly, as God has dealt to each one a measure
of faith. For as we have many members in one body,
but all the members do not have the same function,
so we, being many, are one body in Christ, and
individually members of one another. (Romans 12:1-
5)

When we are not conformed to the self-focused, prideful ways of the secular world, and when we love others the way God loves us, we can then shine the love and light of Christ to those around us. It is a witness and a testimony not only to our own spouse but to the rest of the world, and this is why Jesus Christ says we will be known by our love for one another. *A new commandment I give to you, that you love one another; as I have loved you, that you also love one another. By this all will know that you are My disciples, if you have love for one another. (John 13:34, 35)* When we behave in a loving manner toward the one who is acting unlovable, God softens our hearts toward that person. When we pray for the one who is causing us distress, again, God softens our hearts toward that person. When our intentions are only good toward the one who is treating us badly, God is then invited to change, improve, and strengthen the relationship by the power of His Spirit. *Do not be overcome by evil, but overcome evil with good (Romans 12:21)*

In a nutshell, God commands believers to practice love in the face of hurt feelings; love in the face of disrespect; love in the face of ill treatment; love in the face of trials, stress and tragedy; love in the face of neglect, evil, or hate. Our Lord truly does teach "two wrongs do not make it right" when He tells us not to repay evil with evil. He teaches us to love and be a blessing to others in all diligence and in all sincerity, no matter how we are treated, because that is how we have been treated by Him. We are to look for the good in one another in every situation, rather than focusing on the bad. *Let love be without hypocrisy. Abhor what is evil. Cling to what is good. Be kindly affectionate to one another with brotherly love, in honor giving preference to one another; not lagging in diligence, fervent in spirit, serving the Lord; rejoicing in hope, patient in tribulation, continuing steadfastly in prayer; distributing to the needs of the saints, given to hospitality. Bless those who persecute you; bless and do not curse. Rejoice with those who rejoice, and weep with those who weep. Be of the same mind toward one another. Do not set your mind on high things, but associate with the humble. Do not be wise in your own opinion. Repay no one evil for evil. Have regard for good things in the sight of all men. If it is possible, as much as depends on you, live peaceably with all men. Beloved, do not avenge yourselves, but rather give place to wrath; for it is written, "Vengeance is Mine, I will repay," says the Lord. Therefore, If your enemy is hungry, feed him; If he is thirsty, give him a drink; For in so doing you will heap coals of fire on his head. (Romans 12:9-20)*

Relationship gurus like to tout the "communication" aspect of a marriage relationship as being the ultimate solution to marital discord, however, agape love trumps all communication advice. Agape love turns everything on its head because it serves and loves the spouse even when there is no communication, or even when the communication is unkind and unfruitful. Agape love operates in continual forgiveness and purposeful commitment to the wellbeing of the spouse. There are no grudges when one exhibits such an amazing, freeing love. It is a love that will squelch sin and correct wrong behavior – in both parties. *Hatred stirs up strife, but love covers all sins. (Proverbs 10:2) And above all things have fervent love for one another, for love will cover a multitude of sins. (1st Peter 4:8)*

Communication is certainly useful and necessary between spouses but communication by itself can quickly turn into complaint, insults, accusation, and argument. Sometimes husbands do not want to talk. Sometimes wives have the propensity to talk too much. And sometimes a spouse does not want a response or an opinion, they simply desire a compassionate, listening ear and to know we are there for them. Communication on its own cannot solve marital conflict. Agape love is required.

Holy Spirit-led living compels us to fulfill the needs of our spouse even though it may cost extra time, patience, care, or something we want for ourselves. We are to speak loving words and exhibit compassionate behavior even when we have not been the recipient of those things. *Finally, all of you be of one mind, having compassion for one another; love as brothers, be tenderhearted, be courteous; not returning evil for evil or reviling for reviling, but on the contrary blessing, knowing that you were called to this, that you may inherit a blessing. For He who would love life and see good days, Let him refrain his tongue from evil, and his lips from speaking deceit. Let him turn away from evil and do good; Let him seek peace and pursue it. For the eyes of the LORD are on the righteous, and His ears are open to their prayers; but the face of the LORD is against those who do evil. (1 Peter 3:8-12)* Holy Spirit-led behavior is not argumentative, not prone to anger, does not boast, does not put down or criticize others, and always forgives. *Let no corrupt word proceed out of your mouth, but what is good for necessary edification, that it may impart grace to the hearers. And do not grieve the Holy Spirit of God, by whom you were sealed for the day of redemption. Let all bitterness, wrath, anger, clamor, and evil speaking be put away from you, with all malice. And be kind to one another, tenderhearted, forgiving one another, even as God in Christ forgave you. (Ephesians 4:29-32)*

Chapter Eight

Forgiveness and Marriage

The concept of forgiveness is a key element in a Christian's life because God has forgiven us through our faith in the atoning sacrifice of His only Son, Jesus Christ. Forgiveness is also a fruit of the Holy Spirit and is an action commanded by God to be practiced by the believer. *Let all bitterness, wrath, anger, clamor, and evil speaking be put away from you, with all malice. And be kind to one another, tenderhearted, forgiving one another, even as God in Christ forgave you. (Ephesians 4:31, 32) Therefore, as the elect of God, holy and beloved, put on tender mercies, kindness, humility, meekness, longsuffering; bearing with one another, and forgiving one another, if anyone has a complaint against another; even as Christ forgave you, so you also must do. But above all these things put on love, which is the bond of perfection. And let the peace of God rule in your hearts, to which also you were called in one body; and be thankful. (Colossians 3:12-14)*

Lack of forgiveness is a flesh-driven product of our sin nature and as such it is incredibly harmful to us. When we don't allow ourselves to forgive others we will have no peace in our hearts with regard to that person or that situation. We are warned in the Book of Hebrews about breeding a root of bitterness which will only cause trouble in our lives and actually defiles us from the inside out. *Pursue peace with all people, and holiness, without which no one will see the Lord, looking carefully lest anyone fall short of the grace of God; lest any root of bitterness springing up cause trouble, and by this many become defiled. (Hebrews 12:14, 15)*

The cause of bitterness is an unforgiving attitude. When we do not forgive we open ourselves up to resentment and strife, both of which are strong tools of the devil easily used for destruction. We hurt ourselves far more than we can hurt anyone else with our lack of forgiveness. An unforgiving heart harbors stress and negative feelings which pollute and poison our thoughts, behavior, and speech. The Bible teaches us all our thoughts and speech flows from what is rooted within the heart. *But those things which proceed out of the mouth come from the heart, and they defile a man. For out of the heart proceed evil thoughts, murders, adulteries, fornications, thefts, false witness, [and] blasphemies. (Matthew 15:18, 19)* This is why it is so important to continually dwell in God's Word; daily considering, learning, and memorizing His precepts to ensure the outflow of our heart is God's goodness and righteousness instead of our own sinfulness. *Your word I have hidden in my heart that I might not sin against You. (Psalm 119:11)* The Book of James also commands us to lay aside our tendencies toward wrath and wicked behavior by allowing God's Word to become implanted into our hearts: *So then, my beloved brethren, let every man be swift to hear, slow to speak, slow to wrath, for the wrath of man does not produce the righteousness of God; Therefore lay aside all filthiness and overflow of wickedness, and receive with meekness the implanted word, which is able to save your souls. (James 1:19-21)*

There is a passage in the Book of Matthew which directly discusses the subject of forgiveness. *Then Peter came to Him and said, "Lord, how often shall my brother sin against me and I forgive him? Up to seven times?" Jesus said to him, "I do not say to you, up to seven times, but up to seventy times seven." (Matthew 18:21, 22)* The point of Jesus' response is simply that our attitude must be consistently humble and forgiving toward those who sin against us. We must break our innate tendency to hang on to offended feelings or insulted pride when others say or do wrong things toward us or our loved ones. We are a fallen race living in a fallen world so sinful behavior is most certainly going to happen and negatively affect us. Jesus told us we would have trials and tribulation throughout our lives and yet we act surprised and insulted when we experience such things. How does He tell us to handle it? We must overcome our troubles and trials with a peaceful heart firmly rooted in Jesus Christ. *These things I have spoken to you, that in Me you may have peace. In the world you will have tribulation; but be of good cheer, I have overcome the world. (John 16:33)* Our peace and joy can only come from knowing Jesus Christ and abiding in His Word and His ways. Everything else that happens to us over the course of our lives is trivial in comparison to our personal relationship with Him and therefore should not bother us or move us. *I have set the LORD always before me; because He is at my right hand I shall not be moved. (Psalm 16:8) He only is my rock and my salvation; He is my defense; I shall not be greatly moved. (Psalm 62:2)* The Apostle Paul testifies to the same idea in the Book of Acts; *But none of these things move me; nor do I count my life dear to myself, so that I may finish my race with joy, and the ministry which I received from the Lord Jesus, to testify to the gospel of the grace of God. (Acts 20:24)*

Forgiveness is an expression of agape love. When love is unconditional, forgiveness is a natural resulting outflow of that love. What does Jesus demand of us? *A new commandment I give to you, that you love one another; as I have loved you, that you also love one another. By this all will know that you are My disciples, if you have love for one another.* (John 13:34, 35) The love He speaks of is agape love – the unconditional love Jesus has for us, and the love we are to be living out in our marriages.

Marital strife often is a result of couples not practicing the forgiveness that is a key component of agape love. What could have been a trivial issue quickly sorted out between husband and wife can instead become a long-term offense and relationship barrier when anger, bitterness, and resentment are allowed to build and fester. You may have heard it said we are not to go to bed angry. This holds great truth because it is in fact a biblical teaching found in the Book of Ephesians. *Be angry, and do not sin: do not let the sun go down on your wrath, nor give place to the devil. (Ephesians 4:26, 27)* Unless it is a righteous anger derived from an offense towards God, most anger is a fleshly reaction of our sin nature – our pride or feelings or selfishness took a blow and it makes us angry. God advises we immediately repent of such anger and get rid of it, applying forgiveness where necessary. Look at the words in the above passage, *"nor give place to the devil"*. If we hold onto wrath, nursing it and refusing to forgive, we are giving an opportunity for the devil to attack and injure our marriage relationship. The devil is ceaselessly seeking to destroy all God has created. Marriage is at the top of the list. Any small chink in the marital armor and the devil will find a way to make it bigger and worse. *Be sober, be vigilant; because your adversary the devil walks about like a roaring lion, seeking whom he may devour. (1 Peter 5:8)* The devil will find ways steal your peace, kill your love for one another, and destroy your marriage relationship if you give him an opening to do so. *The thief does not come except to steal, and to kill, and to destroy. (John 10:10)*

Finally, the Bible carries several dire warnings to the believer concerning the lack of forgiveness. *For if you forgive men their trespasses, your heavenly Father will also forgive you. But if you do not forgive men their trespasses, neither will your Father forgive your trespasses. (Matthew 6:14, 15)* Essentially, we are being told if we do not forgive others just as we have been forgiven by God, then God will not forgive us. What a

73

terrible thought! *And whenever you stand praying, if you have anything against anyone, forgive him that your Father in heaven may also forgive you your trespasses. But if you do not forgive, neither will your Father in heaven forgive your trespasses.* (Mark 11:25, 26) The Book of Matthew gives us the following parable which further substantiates the warning: *Therefore the kingdom of heaven is like a certain king who wanted to settle accounts with his servants. And when he had begun to settle accounts, one was brought to him who owed him ten thousand talents. But as he was not able to pay, his master commanded that he be sold, with his wife and children and all that he had, and that payment be made. The servant therefore fell down before him, saying, 'Master, have patience with me, and I will pay you all. Then the master of that servant was moved with compassion, released him, and forgave him the debt. But that servant went out and found one of his fellow servants who owed him a hundred denarii; and he laid hands on him and took him by the throat, saying, 'Pay me what you owe!' So his fellow servant fell down at his feet and begged him, saying, 'Have patience with me, and I will pay you all.' And he would not, but went and threw him into prison till he should pay the debt. So when his fellow servants saw what had been done, they were very grieved, and came and told their master all that had been done. Then his master, after he had called*

*him, said to him, 'You wicked servant! I forgave you
all that debt because you begged me. Should you not
also have had compassion on your fellow servant,
just as I had pity on you?' And his master was angry,
and delivered him to the torturers until he should pay
all that was due to him. So My heavenly Father also
will do to you if each of you, from his heart, does not
forgive his brother his trespasses. (Matthew 18:23-
35)*

Notice in the verses above, we see the
phrase, "if each of you, from his heart, does not
forgive". Forgiveness has to be from our hearts.
It is not something that can be accomplished on
the surface with flippant or insincere words
only. To truly forgive is to stop feeling hurt,
angry, or resentful toward someone because of
something they said or did. It means we treat
them and think of them as if they had done
nothing wrong toward us. Forgiveness is
wiping the slate clean as if the offense never
happened, and also involves choosing not to
punish or take revenge on someone who has
sinned against you. If we find ourselves in a
situation where hurt or angry feelings simply
are not going away and therefore having
forgiveness seems unattainable, we must pray
for God to give us the ability to forgive. He will
answer that prayer, for it is His will that we

forgive others. This is especially important within the parameters of marriage. Because husbands and wives live in very close contact and fellowship with one another on a daily basis, they are bound to be subject to numerous moments of each other's shortcomings, failures and sins. Without a humble, committed, agape level of love producing a continual outpouring of patience and forgiveness, marriage relationships will falter and become open to deterioration and damage over time.

Chapter Nine

Marriage Wisdom: The Book of Proverbs

The Book of Proverbs was written by the wisest man on earth, King Solomon. We are told his wisdom was a God-given gift never equaled again on earth. Solomon was also a man to whom God gave not only wisdom but immense wealth, ruling power, and the freedom and overall capability to pursue every possible experience in life in order to test out the truths of God's wisdom and the meaning of human existence. One of the very first truths we can find in the Book of Proverbs is the following statement: *The fear of the LORD is the beginning of knowledge, but fools despise wisdom and instruction. (Proverbs 1:7)* Solomon reiterates this first proverb at the end of the Book of Ecclesiastes: *Let us hear the conclusion of the whole matter: Fear God and keep His commandments, for this is man's all. (Ecclesiastes 12:13)* When we truly fear and revere God as our living, active, ruling and reigning Creator and Savior, we will have a deep desire to learn Who He is and follow His commands regarding all things in life, including marriage. If we have a big enough concept of God we will understand He has the only wisdom worth hearing and the only instructions worth following. We can quickly reach the conclusion we must be continually discovering what His Word tells us and we also understand it will take the rest of our earthly lives to grow our faith, mature in His wisdom, and work out our own sanctification. A good starting point in anyone's walk of faith is to memorize Proverbs 1:7 and move forward in learning from there.

As believers, we must come to a paradigm shift of realizing our own ideas and perceptions are often very wrong when held under the scrutiny of God's commands and precepts. His ways are not our ways, His thoughts are not our thoughts. *For My thoughts are not your thoughts, nor are your ways My ways,"* *says the LORD. For as the heavens are higher than the earth, so are My ways higher than your ways, and My thoughts than your thoughts. (Isaiah 55:8, 9)* Because of this, the Bible states we must trust in God rather than in our own understanding. *Trust in the LORD with all your heart, and lean not on your own understanding; in all your ways acknowledge Him, and He shall direct your paths (Proverbs 3:5, 6).* If we want to pursue God's very best will for us we must learn to trust in His ways, seek His wisdom, and allow our life's paths be directed by Him via His Word, His spiritual promptings, and our prayer life with Him.

Foundationally, the above passages bring us back to why is it so incredibly important to know what God teaches about love and marriage, husbands and wives, and spiritual living versus fleshly living. Without an active knowledge of God's Word, the paths most marriages take are bound to be crooked, confusing, and ultimately lead to failure. Without God's wisdom we are lost, in the dark, and directionless in every facet of life. The secular world thinks placing emphasis on the pursuits of self-love, self-esteem, and self-gratification should be the primary goals of human life. The rejection of God and His Word has resulted in an ever-increasing tide of godlessness and immorality which has singlehandedly erased all knowledge of God's foundational principles regarding love, marriage, and family. The all-too common struggles of single parenting, divorce, adultery, substance abuse, joblessness, anxiety, depression, suicide, murder, gender confusion, sexual immorality, and a myriad of additional societal afflictions are the direct result of living far from the knowledge and influence of God. *Do not be wise in your own eyes; Fear the LORD and depart from evil. It will be health to your flesh, and strength to your bones. (Proverbs 3:7, 8)* Without God's teachings and truths we are indeed destined to be physically, emotionally, spiritually, and culturally unhealthy and weak; and within the context of this book, this consequence applies very much so to marriage.

The Lord commands husbands in Proverbs 5 to stay faithful to their spouses using poetic verbiage about wells and cisterns. *Drink water from your own cistern, and running water from your own well. Should your fountains be dispersed abroad, Streams of water in the streets? Let them be only your own, and not for strangers with you. (Proverbs 5:15-17)* The passage reinforces the understanding that God's purpose for marriage is for one man and one woman to be committed solely to one another for a lifetime. This thought develops further on in the passage by encouraging the husband to have pleasure, joy and great satisfaction with his wife, being wholly captivated by her love for him. *Let your fountain be blessed, and rejoice with the wife of your youth. As a loving deer and a graceful doe, let her breasts satisfy you at all times; and always be enraptured with her love. (Proverbs 5:18, 19)* Such teachings fly in the face of modern day relationship perceptions which boast of multiple sexual partners and numerous uncommitted sexual experiences as being normal and healthy. Yet we see in the Bible that God continually promotes the oneness of husbands and wives within the union of marriage as being sacred and of great value. He also conversely holds any kind physical union outside of marriage as being wrong and very harmful. Today's world no longer has knowledge of such truths and because of the resulting depraved lifestyles our families, cities, and nations are self-destructing and decaying from within.

Further on in Proverbs we begin to see many wisdom verses which focus upon the sin of pride and the incessant tendency we all have to run our mouths, making bad situations and struggling relationships worse. It is a great idea to set our minds on the following verses and commit them to memory for the sake of taking every thought captive and bringing all our words and actions under the obedience of Jesus

Christ, especially in times of relational duress or argument.

The fear of the LORD is to hate evil; Pride and arrogance and the evil way and the perverse mouth I hate. *(Proverbs 8:13)* The word "perverse" is defined as 'obstinate, willful, stubborn, unreasonable, rebellious, inappropriate, irrational, vexatious'. If a conversation escalates into a disagreement, and that disagreement then develops into an argument, you can be sure a perverse mouth is at work in one or both partners. We must learn to tame our tongues and bring every conversation under the light and lens of the Holy Spirit; asking what Jesus would have us say or do rather than reacting in our flesh with a *perverse mouth.*

When pride comes, then comes shame; but with the humble is wisdom. *(Proverbs 11:2)* The overriding sentiment continues to circle back to the constant need for humility. According to God, being humble is the wise route, the commanded route, and the conflict-diffusing route. *In the multitude of words sin is not lacking, but he who restrains his lips is wise. (Proverbs 10:19)* This verse is literally teaching that the more one speaks, the bigger the possibility of sinning with our words. The Book of James has great teachings on practicing self-control when it comes to what we say. Remember the command found in James 1:19; *So then, my beloved brethren, let every man be swift to hear, slow to speak, slow to wrath.* Too often we can have such a tendency to speak before thinking, talk without wanting to listen, and become angry in the heat of the moment. God knows this well and addresses it several times and in different ways throughout Scripture. *For we all stumble in many things. If anyone does not stumble in word, he is a perfect man, able also to bridle the whole body. Indeed, we put bits in horses' mouths that they may obey us, and we turn their whole body. Look also at ships: although they are so large and are driven by fierce winds, they are turned by a very small rudder wherever the pilot desires. Even so the tongue is a little member and boasts great things. See how great a forest a little fire kindles! And the tongue is a fire, a world of iniquity. The tongue is so set among our members that it defiles the whole body, and sets on fire the course of nature; and it is set on fire by hell. For every kind of beast and bird, of reptile and creature of the sea, is tamed and has been tamed by mankind. But no man can tame the tongue. It is an unruly evil, full of deadly poison. (James 3:2-8)* When we read a teaching like this, we can see how destructive our words can be.

From such passages we understand the less we say, and the more we think and pray before we say it, the better off everyone is. We need to keep these things in mind when communicating with all people, however it is especially important to do so when speaking with your spouse. Again, it is so crucial that the words we use with our marriage partners are those which bless, build up, edify and strengthen. We cannot be in the practice of carelessly flinging around criticisms, judgments and words which tear down our spouses.

When God says through James, "*See how great a forest a little fire kindles!*" He is teaching us how far-reaching and monumentally destructive our words can be. Words spoken out loud cannot be retracted, for they cannot be unheard. This thought is emphasized in the following Proverb: *There is one who speaks like the piercings of a sword, but the tongue of the wise promotes health. (Proverbs 12:18)* Are we verbally stabbing and injuring others like the piercings of a sword? Or are we wisely promoting health and peace? *A soft answer turns away wrath, but a harsh word stirs up anger. (Proverbs 15:1)* Our Lord is so incredibly consistent in showing us throughout Scripture how our words either build up or tear down; make things worse or make them better. *Pleasant words are like a honeycomb, Sweetness to the soul and health to the bones. (Proverbs 16:24)* What we say is a choice; a Spirit-led choice or a flesh-driven choice. In our marriages especially, we must choose wisely.

The Book of Proverbs also contains special commentary dealing with speech as it pertains to a bad habit of many wives – a subject which we have already covered earlier in this book. Since God takes the time to point out the issue in more than one place, it is good to remind ourselves of the teaching behind the passages. God is very noticeably pointing out that certain wives are prone to nag, complain, and criticize their husbands in a continual, irritating manner. Again, we discovered this tendency is part of the curse given to women in Genesis 3, in that they will want to rule over their husbands even though their husbands are commanded by God to rule over them instead. The Book of Proverbs displays the unwanted behavior in a very descriptive style in the following manner:

1) *Better to dwell in a corner of a housetop, than in a house shared with a contentious woman. (Proverbs 21:9)*

2) *It is better to dwell in a corner of a housetop, than in a house shared with a contentious woman. (Proverbs 25:4)*

3) *A continual dripping on a very rainy day and a contentious woman are alike; whoever restrains her restrains the wind, and grasps oil with his right hand. (Proverbs 27:15,16)*

4) *An excellent wife is the crown of her husband, but she who causes shame is like rottenness in his bones. (Proverbs 12:4)*

The Holy Spirit has corrected me and my own tongue on this issue ever since I became aware of the above verses and He will likely have to continue working with me the rest of my life. I find myself literally in the act of starting to speak a thought out loud to my husband when the Spirit checks me, causing me to pause as God shows me I was going to say something totally unnecessary and downright critical. Just as everything is on our spiritual walk, this taming of the tongue is a continual process, but it is most definitely one worth learning and practicing! We must persistently strive to be led by the Spirit and not ruled by our sin nature in all facets of life. If we do not purposefully discipline ourselves we will be left unprotected and open to all manner of assaults from the world, from our flesh, and from the devil. *Whoever has no rule over his own spirit is like a city broken down, without walls. (Proverbs 25:8)*

Finally, there is a beautiful verse in Proverbs which can be a source of great encouragement to those husbands and wives who may not have much in material possession, but what they do have is the fear of the Lord, salvation through Jesus Christ, and the peaceful agape love of God in their marriage. *Better is a little with the fear of the LORD, than great treasure with trouble. Better is a dinner of herbs where love is, than a fatted calf with hatred. (Proverbs 15:16, 17)* The picture here is of a prosperous, healthy, loving, peaceful, and Spirit-filled life and marriage which is such an enormous blessing that a humble, limited dinner of herbs and vegetables is far preferable to great material bounty and a rich steak feast on the table in the home of a godless and strife-stricken marriage. The wisdom of God truly surpasses the wisdom of man on every level, and when we embed His teachings such as those found in the Book of Proverbs into our lives and ways of thinking, we will find God gives great spiritual blessing, sure direction, straight paths for our feet, and peaceful hearts. *I will bring the blind by a way they did not know; I will lead them in paths they have not known. I will make darkness light before them, and crooked places straight. These things I will do for them, and not forsake them. (Isaiah 42:16)*

Chapter Ten

Marriage and Our Personal Relationship with Jesus

Unless the LORD builds the house, they labor in vain who build it; unless the LORD guards the city, the watchman stays awake in vain. (Psalm 127:1) The foundation of all things is Jesus Christ. If we do not build on that foundation, our life-long efforts and accomplishments will be without meaning, without substance, and will not endure. We must seek to build our own relationship with God before doing anything else in life, or we will surely fail in all things. *But seek first the kingdom of God and His righteousness, and all these things shall be added to you. (Matthew 6:33)* The preceding verses to the above passage in the Book of Matthew discuss Jesus' commands against worrying about life, food, clothing, and the future. He tells the disciples they are not to concern themselves with worrying about such things. He instructs them to instead direct their focus on seeking the kingdom of God and His righteousness. In doing so, they will find God provides for them all that He deems necessary and beneficial for their daily lives.

Now, obviously this doesn't mean we should sit around praying and reading our Bibles while doing nothing productive to earn our way in this world. We are warned in several places throughout Scripture not to be lazy or idle but to work hard in all things, as unto the Lord. *If anyone will not work, neither shall he eat. (2 Thessalonians 3:10) Go to the ant, you sluggard! Consider her ways and be wise (Proverbs 6:6) And whatever you do, do it heartily, as to the Lord and not to men, knowing that from the Lord you will receive the reward of the inheritance; for you serve the Lord Christ. (Colossians 3:23, 24)* The point being, we are simply to put Jesus in front of our eyes each and every day, living for His purposes, seeking His guidance, and fellowshipping with Him in thought and prayer as we go about our business. This is what it means to be seeking first the kingdom of heaven. If we are daily nourishing our spirits with Scripture and cherishing our spiritual relationship with God, we will find ourselves on well-lit paths. *Your word is a lamp to my feet and a light to my path. (Psalm 119:105)* All we put our minds and hands to will prosper. *Blessed is the man who walks not in the counsel of the ungodly, nor stands in the path of sinners, nor sits in the seat of the scornful; but his delight is in the law of the LORD, and in His law he meditates day and night. He shall be like a tree planted by the rivers of water that brings forth its fruit in its season, whose leaf also shall not wither; and whatever he does shall prosper. (Psalm 1:1-3)*

Our number one goal in life must be to attend to our own, one-on-one vertical relationship with God before we attend to anything or anyone else. All other relationships are secondary, and in fact, unless our vertical relationship with the Lord is on track, our horizontal relationships with others will not be on track. This truth is especially crucial as it pertains to the marriage relationship. Numerous times in both Old and New Testaments we see the instruction: *You shall love the LORD your God with all your heart, with all your soul, and with all your strength. (Deuteronomy 6:5)* This is our greatest command, and it clearly is about our own personal, vertical relationship with God. Secondarily, the instruction given by Jesus which follows this great command is concerning our horizontal relationships with others: *And you shall love the LORD your God with all your heart, with all your soul, with all your mind, and with all your strength. This is the first commandment. And the second, like it, is this: You shall love your neighbor as yourself. There is no other commandment greater than these. (Mark 12:30, 31)*

We simply cannot be a blessing to our spouse or anyone else if we are not in fellowship with the Lord. The only way we can be properly equipped to engage in the agape love of marriage and Holy Spirit-led living is if we are born again and living out our faith daily seeking God's face. The humble, loving, selfless, spirit-led behavior God requires us to exhibit in the bond of marriage and in unity amongst our brothers and sisters in Christ cannot be practiced if it is not flowing out of us by the power of the Holy Spirit. The following instruction is an incredible summary of how God expects us to conduct ourselves, giving the reason why we are able to do so at the very end – because we have believed in the atoning death of Jesus Christ and therefore we have been made spiritually alive and empowered by the Holy Spirit. *Finally, all of you be of one mind, having compassion for one another; love as brothers, be tenderhearted, be courteous; not returning evil for evil or reviling for reviling, but on the contrary blessing, knowing that you were called to this, that you may inherit a blessing. For "He who would love life and see good days, Let him refrain his tongue from evil, and his lips from speaking deceit. Let him* turn away from evil and do good; Let him seek peace and pursue it. For the eyes of the LORD are on the righteous, and His ears are open to their prayers; but the face of the LORD is against those who do evil." And who is he who will harm you if you become followers of what is good? But even if you should suffer for righteousness' sake, you are blessed. "And do not be afraid of their threats, nor be troubled." But sanctify the Lord God in your hearts, and always be ready to give a defense to everyone who asks you a reason for the hope that is in you, with meekness and fear; having a good conscience, that when they defame you as evildoers, those who revile your good conduct in Christ may be ashamed. For it is better, if it is the will of God, to suffer for doing good than for doing evil. For Christ also suffered once for sins, the just for the unjust, that He might bring us to God, being put to death in the flesh but made alive by the Spirit. (1 Peter 3:8-18)

We must continually be dying to self and allowing Jesus Christ and the power of His love to live in us and through us. *I have been crucified with Christ; it is no longer I who live, but Christ lives in me; and the life which I now live in the flesh I live by faith in the Son of God, who loved me and gave Himself for me. (Galatians 2:20)* This is about shining His light and His love toward our spouse and everyone in our sphere of influence. The origination of agape love is God. He *is* love and since we are His image bearers, He commands us to practice that love also. *Beloved, let us love one another, for love is of God; and everyone who loves is born of God and knows God. (1 John 4:7) And this is His commandment: that we should believe on the name of His Son Jesus Christ and love one another, as He gave us commandment. (1 John 3:23)*

We can only practice this kind of love if we are living in faith as believers in Jesus Christ and His work on the cross. *For God so loved the world that He gave His only begotten Son, that whoever believes in Him should not perish but have everlasting life. (John 3:16)* We are taught throughout Scripture *that Christ died for our sins according to the Scriptures, and that He was buried, and that He rose again the third day according to the Scriptures (1 Corinthians 15:3, 4)* If we believe these things, we will be born again and have our sins forgiven; enabling us to begin a living, active, spiritual relationship with God here on earth and into eternity. My final encouragement to you is to please make sure you have taken this first step of faith in Jesus Christ before attempting to live out the rest of the biblical marital instruction in this book, or you will fail trying to do it in your own power. Submit your life to the lordship of Jesus Christ today. Ask

Him to forgive you of your innate sin of rebellion against God and His purposes, and make you a new creation, sealing you with His Holy Spirit and giving you His merciful and gracious gifts of eternal salvation, sanctification, and redemption. Only when you take this step can you move forward in the joy of a biblical marriage relationship with your spouse.

He has shown you, O man, what is good; and what does the LORD require of you but to do justly, to love mercy, and to walk humbly with your God? (Micah 6:8)

APPENDIX A

Biblical Principles of Divorce

Although this book was written so those who read it can learn how to have a joy- filled, loving, and peaceable biblical marriage, I do feel it is important to discuss what God teaches about divorce. Divorce happens so often in our world, and it seems evident most people – including Christians – do not know what the Bible actually teaches about the matter. So let's address the issue. What does God have to say about divorce? The Book of Deuteronomy has specific rules about situations in the culture of that era in which a man may or may not divorce his wife, however, we know divorce itself was never God's original intent nor is it His best plan for mankind.

Remember, the original purpose of marriage was to bless men and women with a wonderful gift of emotional and physical security, human companionship, a means for procreation, and enjoyment of sexual intimacy within the parameters of a solemn, lifetime commitment made by both partners. God's objective on this issue has not changed and will never change. *For I am the LORD, I do not change.* *(Malachi 3:6)* In fact, we are told in both the Old and New Testament God hates divorce and He commands it should not happen. The Book of Malachi has a powerful passage which must not be looked upon lightly:

So He [God] does not regard the offering anymore, nor receives it with goodwill from your hands. Yet you say, "For what reason?" Because the LORD has been witness between you and the wife of your youth, with whom you have dealt treacherously; yet she is your companion and your wife by covenant. But did He not make them one, having a remnant of the Spirit? And why one? He seeks godly offspring. Therefore take heed to your spirit, and let none deal treacherously with the wife of his youth. For the LORD God of Israel says that He hates divorce for it covers one's garment with violence," says the LORD of hosts. "Therefore take heed to your spirit that you do not deal treacherously." (Malachi 2:13-16)

The wording of this passage is heart wrenchingly beautiful – "divorce covers one's garment with violence". When husbands and wives separate from each other, it not only causes emotional and spiritual violence to both spouses, but also results in a spiritual violence toward God and His protective covering of marriage over the husband and wife. Marriage is a special, covenant relationship given to men and women by God and instituted for the benefit and blessing of the human race. God provides marriage as a covering or "garment" which is placed over the husband and wife and sets them apart in a holy, sacred union which is undefiled and honorable. Divorce covers that garment with violence. God does not want such a violence to happen to His gift and covering, consequently He commands against it. *So then, they are no longer two but one flesh. Therefore what God has joined together, let not man separate. (Matthew 19:6) (Mark 10:9)*

It is only because of human sin, the hardness of hearts, and the generations of people who no longer carry within themselves a proper fear of the Lord that God made provisions for divorce through the laws given to Moses. Unfortunately, just like today, during the time of Moses the use of divorce to deal with marital dissatisfaction became a common and trivial practice. Husbands were given over to divorcing their wives for the tiniest infractions or offenses and as such they were leading lives of continual remarriage and adulterous behavior. Their hearts were not turned toward

God and His commands on this matter, but rather toward selfish desires and lawlessness. When Jesus Christ began His ministry He rebuked the religious leaders for this very thing.

The Pharisees also came to Him, testing Him, and saying to Him, "Is it lawful for a man to divorce his wife for just any reason?" And He answered and said to them, "Have you not read that He who made them at the beginning 'made them male and female, and said, 'For this reason a man shall leave his father and mother and be joined to his wife, and the two shall become one flesh'? So then, they are no longer two but one flesh. Therefore what God has joined together, let not man separate. They said to Him, "Why then did Moses command to give a certificate of divorce, and to put her away?" He said to them, "Moses, because of the hardness of your hearts, permitted you to divorce your wives, but from the beginning it was not so. And I say to you, whoever divorces his wife, except for sexual immorality, and marries another, commits adultery; and whoever marries her who is divorced commits adultery. (Matthew 19:3-9)

The Pharisees came and asked Him, "Is it lawful for a man to divorce his wife?" testing Him. And He answered and said to them, "What did Moses command you?" They said, "Moses permitted a man to write a certificate of divorce, and to dismiss her." And Jesus answered and said to them, "Because of the hardness of your heart he wrote you this precept. "But from the beginning of the creation, God 'made them male and female. 'For this reason a man shall leave his father and mother and be joined to his wife and the two shall become one flesh'; so then they are no longer two, but one flesh. Therefore what God has joined together, let not man separate." In the house His disciples also asked Him again about the same matter. So He said to them, "Whoever divorces his wife and marries another commits adultery against her. And if a woman divorces her husband and marries another, she commits adultery. (Mark 10:2-12)

Divorce was never God's original plan for the human race. Look at the words of Jesus again in the above Matthew 19 verses: *"From the beginning it was not so."* God's best plan was for men and women to make a sacred and holy covenant with one another in marriage, in order to be set apart for only each other the duration of their earthly lives. Yet as time passed, in His great mercy He put into place a few exceptions, fully knowing our sin nature and our propensity to turn away from His will. According to what we read in Scripture, God determined one reason in which divorce is justifiable is in the case of unrepentant sexual immorality or adultery. *Furthermore it has been* said, 'Whoever divorces his wife, let him give her a certificate of divorce.' But I [Jesus] say to you that whoever divorces his wife for any reason except sexual immorality causes her to commit adultery; and whoever marries a woman who is divorced commits adultery. (Matthew 5:31,32)

This is not to say a marriage that has suffered an adulterous indiscretion cannot be saved, for indeed it can, as long as the adultery stops and both spouses recommit themselves to one another and to the Lord in a biblical manner. However, in the case where a spouse continually and unrepentantly commits acts of sexual immorality or will not cease an extramarital affair, God is merciful and tells us a divorce may take place without His condemnation.

A second provision for divorce can be made in the case of a marriage where one of the spouses is not a Christian and the other one is, causing some type of unsolvable conflict. Let's begin examining this premise with a very strongly worded command found in the Book of 2nd Corinthians:

Do not be unequally yoked together with unbelievers. For what fellowship has righteousness with lawlessness? And what communion has light

101

with darkness? (2 Corinthians 6:14). Paul had already given additional insight on this particular topic in his first letter to the Corinthians, explaining God's best plan is for wives and husbands not to divorce one another, but if they do, they are supposed to remain single or else seek reconciliation. Furthermore, in the case of spiritually unequal marriages we are told if an unbelieving spouse is willing to stay married to their believing spouse, the believing spouse should not divorce him or her because they may be able to influence and win the unbelieving partner over to the Lord with their godly conduct and additionally, their children will be holy. However, if the unbelieving partner wants to divorce the believing one, God will allow it:

Now to the married I command, yet not I but the Lord: A wife is not to depart from her husband. But even if she does depart, let her remain unmarried or be reconciled to her husband. And a husband is not to divorce his wife. But to the rest I, not the Lord, say: If any brother [believer] has a wife who does not believe, and she is willing to live with him, let him not divorce her. And a woman [believer] who has a husband who does not believe, if he is willing to live with her, let her not divorce him. For the unbelieving husband is sanctified by the wife, and the unbelieving wife is sanctified by the husband; otherwise your children would be unclean, but now they are holy. But if the unbeliever departs, let him depart; a brother or a sister is not under bondage in such cases. But God has called us to peace. For how do you know, O wife, whether you will save your husband? Or how do you know, O husband, whether you will save your wife? (1 Corinthians 7:10-16)

Such teachings in the above passages indicate the importance of believers seeking a marriage relationship only with other believers. When a believing, god-fearing man or woman becomes yoked together with an unbelieving spouse, they are signing themselves up for spiritual disaster as well as inevitable marital disaster down the road. Again, read the command: *Do not be unequally yoked together with unbelievers. For what fellowship has righteousness with lawlessness? And what communion has light with darkness? And what accord has Christ with Belial? Or what part has a believer with an unbeliever?* (2 Corinthians 6:14, 15) Christians have nothing in common with nonbelievers and therefore have no business becoming entangled in intimate relationships with them. The Christian has a moral compass grounded in the Word of God which the unbeliever does not have. Their worldviews are intrinsically disparate, their behaviors will be opposing, and their goals, focus, and living

103

habits are inherently incongruent on every level. As the Bible simply states, Jesus cannot be in agreement with the devil, light has no fellowship with darkness, and believers have no part with unbelievers.

The believer's spirit has been born again into a living relationship with God through faith in Jesus Christ and what He has done on the cross. As a result, the believer has been given the gift of the Holy Spirit, through which he or she can commune with God. *And when He had said this, He breathed on them, and said to them, "Receive the Holy Spirit. (John 20:22) Then Peter said to them, "Repent, and let every one of you be baptized in the name of Jesus Christ for the remission of sins; and you shall receive the gift of the Holy Spirit. (Acts 2:38) Now hope does not disappoint, because the love of God has been poured out in our hearts by the Holy Spirit who was given to us. (Romans 5:5) Or do you not know that your body is the temple of the Holy Spirit who is in you, whom you have from God, and you are not your own?(1 Corinthians 6:19) In Him you also trusted, after you heard the word of truth, the gospel of your salvation; in whom also, having believed, you were sealed with the Holy Spirit of promise, who is the guarantee of our inheritance until the redemption of the purchased possession, to the praise of His glory. (Ephesians 1:13, 14)*

Conversely, an unbelieving partner is still in a state of spiritual death, and not able to be in complete fellowship (body-mind-spirit) with a believing partner. They can relate to each other on two levels only – through their bodies and their minds; but they can have no relationship spiritually, which is the most important level. Despite this frightening disparity, many Christians allow themselves to fall in love with unbelieving partners, hoping to lead them to seek Jesus and find their own faith. This certainly can happen, and the 1st Corinthians passage clearly indicates God can indeed work in such a manner; *For how do you know, O wife, whether you will save your husband? Or how do you know, O husband, whether you will save your wife? (1 Corinthians 7:16)* But it would take a very patient, spiritually strong, ceaselessly praying spouse to withstand the trials and temptations such an unequal relationship causes.

The reality is, more often than not the believing spouse becomes pulled into a spiritually compromised, backslidden, worldly existence right alongside the secular lifestyle of the unbelieving partner. In essence, the believing spouse is eventually influenced to live for the lust of the eyes, lust of the flesh, and the pride of life, habitually disregarding a daily relationship with Jesus Christ in favor of living after the manner of the unbelieving spouse. Church attendance drops, bible reading stops, prayer becomes a sporadic duty, and the children end up being raised in a secular fashion, having no spiritually consistent parental behavior to emulate.

In such a case it would have been better for the couple to not have gotten married, for now the spiritual relationship between the Christian spouse and Jesus is at risk, and as a result, their eternity is at risk. This is a very serious matter, and we must realize God's commands and rules are written for good reason. He knows what will lead us astray and He knows what will protect us. Being unequally yoked usually will lead a Christian down a worldly, spiritually dangerous road. God is always working to protect our relationship with Him as well as preserve our eternal wellbeing, and as such we should revere and fear His biblical commands in such a manner that we obey them wholeheartedly.

The fear of the LORD is the beginning of wisdom; a good understanding have all those who do His commandments. (Psalm 111:10) The fear of the Lord is indeed the beginning of wisdom, no matter the subject or situation. *Therefore, my beloved, as you have always obeyed, not as in my presence only, but now much more in my absence, work out your own salvation with fear and trembling (Philippians 2:12)* There are things we can do in this life which will put both our relationship with God and our eternal salvation at risk. If there were not, we would have no need for any of God's teachings on how to live a life worthy of our calling, and there would be no need for us to faithfully abide in Him and strive to continually take heed of His warnings.

Throughout the Bible we see God repeating His most important command to the human race; that our love for God must come before everyone and everything else:

1) *You shall love the LORD your God with all your heart, with all your soul, and with all your strength. (Deuteronomy 6:5)*
2) *And you shall love the LORD your God with all your heart, with all your soul, with all your mind, and with all your strength. This is the first commandment (Mark 12:30)*
3) *You shall love the LORD your God with all your heart, with all your soul, with all your strength, and with all your mind, and your neighbor as yourself. (Luke 10:27*

Nothing and no one should come between you and your relationship with God. During His earthly ministry Jesus taught that if anyone places more importance on their relationship with family members or a loved one than on Him, he or she is not worthy of Him: *He who loves father or mother more than Me is not worthy of Me. And he who loves son or daughter more than Me is not worthy of Me (Matthew 10:37)* It is from this perspective God allows divorce between an unbelieving spouse and a spouse who is a follower of Jesus Christ. The Bible appears to further strengthen this position in the following passage: *And everyone who has left houses or brothers or sisters or father or mother or wife or children or lands, for My name's sake, shall receive a hundredfold, and inherit eternal life. (Matthew 19:29)* This verse specifically mentions wives along with the other family members.

I cannot be dogmatic on this, but in terms of divorce, this passage in Matthew seems to indicate a husband or wife may need to leave their spouse for the sake of their personal relationship with Jesus – the assumption being that the unequal marriage relationship in some way is drastically hindering or adversely affecting the faith and spiritual walk of the believing spouse. God's primary concern for us is our relationship with Him. If unbelieving spouses or family members are a dangerous obstacle to our walk with Jesus Christ, we must humbly seek God's will on the matter and pray for His clear guidance. It is His first, best choice that we stay and work on our marriage. But, if the relationship is physically, emotionally or spiritually harmful, He may well direct us to leave it, for He wants us to be at peace on this matter. *But God has called us to peace. (1 Corinthians 7:15)* In summary, while God hates divorce, it is clear that because of our fallen nature He has made specific provisions for allowable divorces in the cases of unrepentant adultery, and unequally yoked marital relationships.

The End

Made in the USA
Columbia, SC
03 May 2022

59848678R00067